FREEDOM BABY ABC
Gun Safety from Ammo to X-Ring

written & illustrated by Jane Sharpe

other books by Jane Sharpe: Gun Safety Activity Book for Kids, the Companion to Freedom Baby ABC

Crunchy Mama ABC, from Amber to Zinc
Kitchen Helper ABC, Cooking with Kids from Apron to Zester

Coloring & Activity Book for Crunchy Mama ABC
Cooking Skills Coloring & Activity Book

Record Book for Children with Complex Medical Care: manage the data associated with chronic conditions and congenital disorders

Record Book for Children with Complex Behavioral Needs: manage the data associated with neurodevelopmental and developmental disabilities, including Autism

Investigating the Cause: Recording Your Child's Flare-Ups, Reactions, Symptoms, and Care

Planning and Tracking Your Detox; Cleanse Journal for Symptoms and Healing

<u>Freedom Baby ABC, Gun Safety from Ammo to X-ring</u>
written and illustrated by Jane Sharpe

Second edition, December 2023
ISBN 979-887-2690-658

Text and images copyright 2021
All rights reserved

special thanks to @Riley_TXShooter

www.JaneSharpe.com

Tom Claycomb, AMMOLAND SHOOTING SPORTS NEWS

> "The author Jane Sharpe is putting boundaries back to where they were 60 years ago, before the thought police and reshape-America socialists started to reprogram everyone."

> "Freedom Baby ABC sets a foundation for personal responsibility and perpetual growth."
>
> Matt Beaudreau, President, Acton Academy; Co-Founder, ApogeeStrong.com

DR'GO

> "Freedom Baby ABC is a lovely way to introduce toddlers to the alphabet and to firearms along with the rest of their world."
>
> —Robert B. Young, MD Executive Editor, Doctors for Responsible Gun Ownership

> "Every home that has a firearm needs to make sure that every family member knows how to handle a gun safely, and this little ABC book reinforces commonsense safety rules."
>
> —Lisa Bedford, author of "Survival Mom"

Aa

ammo

Bb
brass

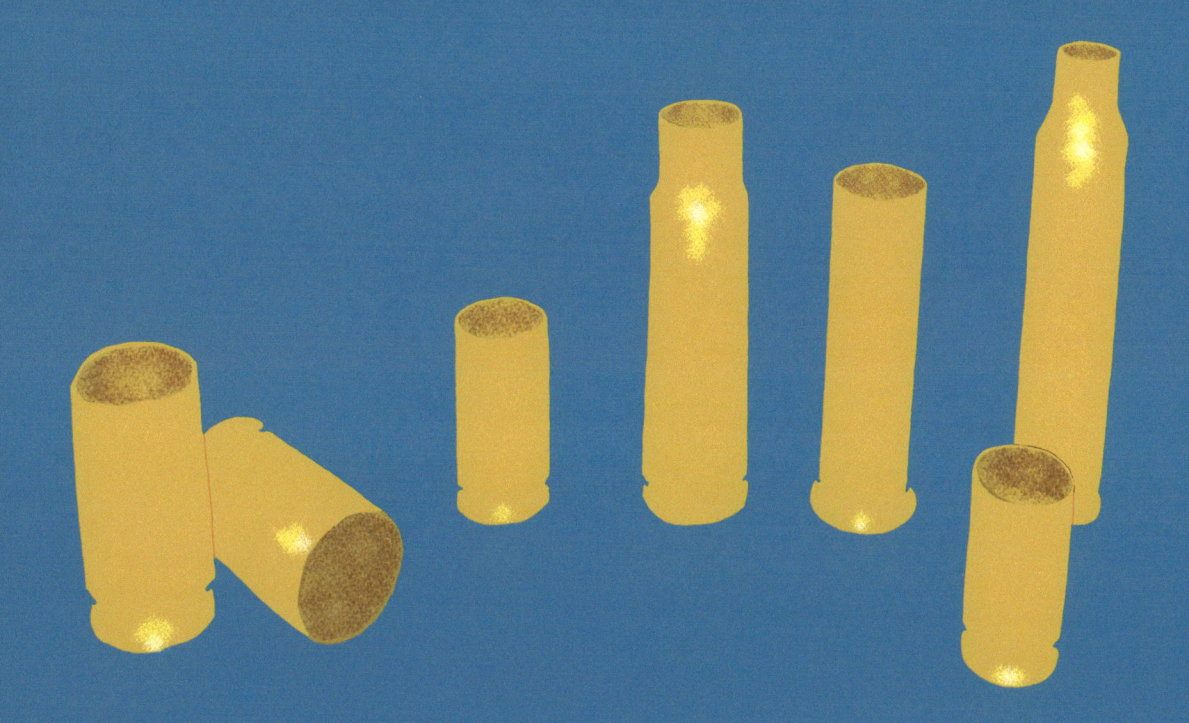

Cc
clay pigeons

Dd
we have a duty to defend

Ee
ear protection

Ff
freedom

I.
II. keep and bear arms
III.
IV.
V.
VI.
VII.
VIII.
IX.
X.

Gg
guns are a tool

Hh
hunting

Ii
improve

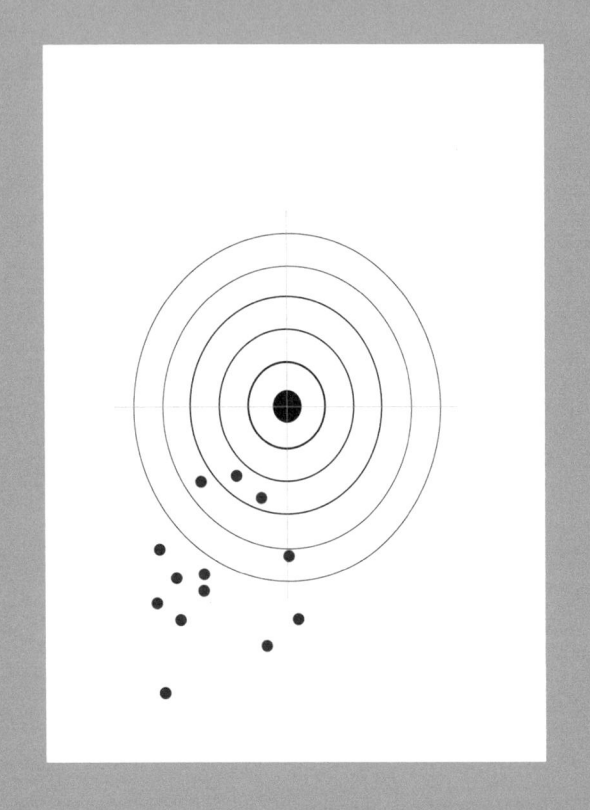

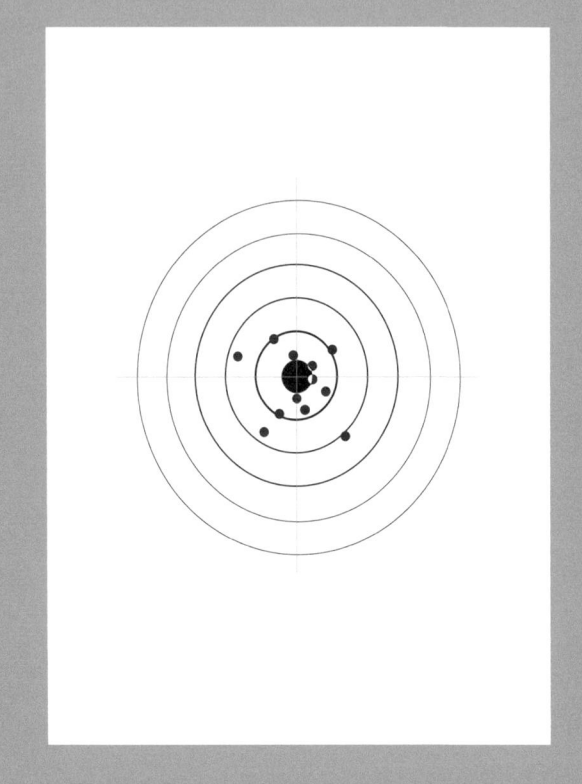

Jj
jacketed

Kk
keep guns locked up

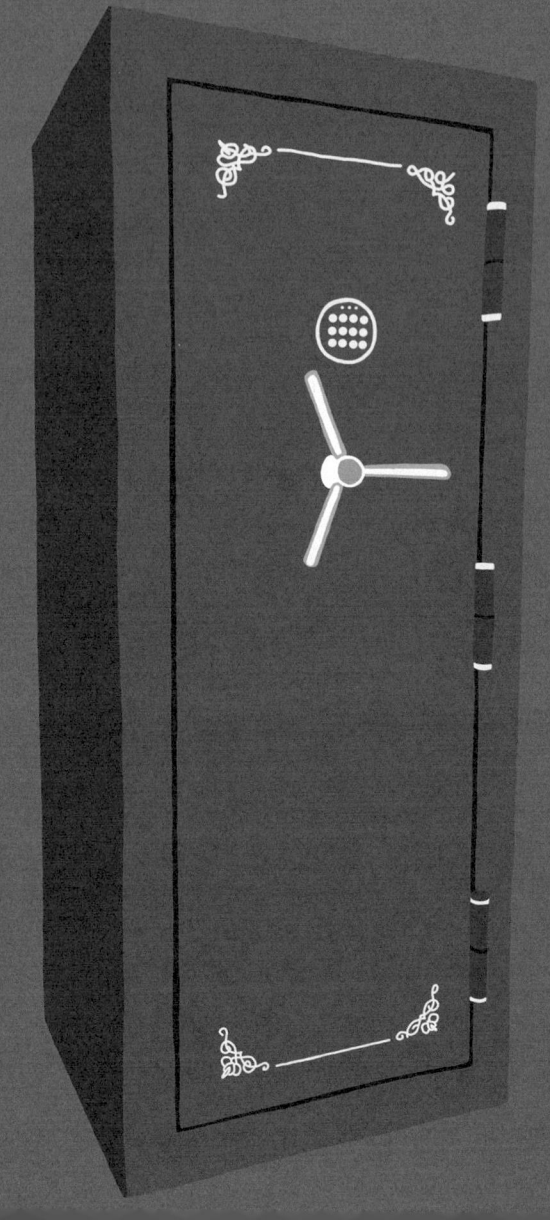

Ll
lead

Mm
magazine

NEVER
never!
never
play with guns!

Oo
optics

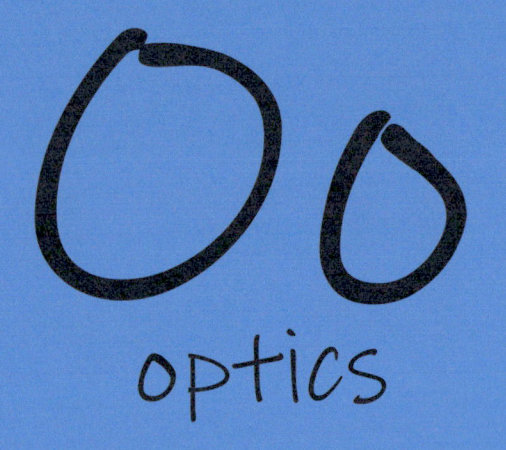

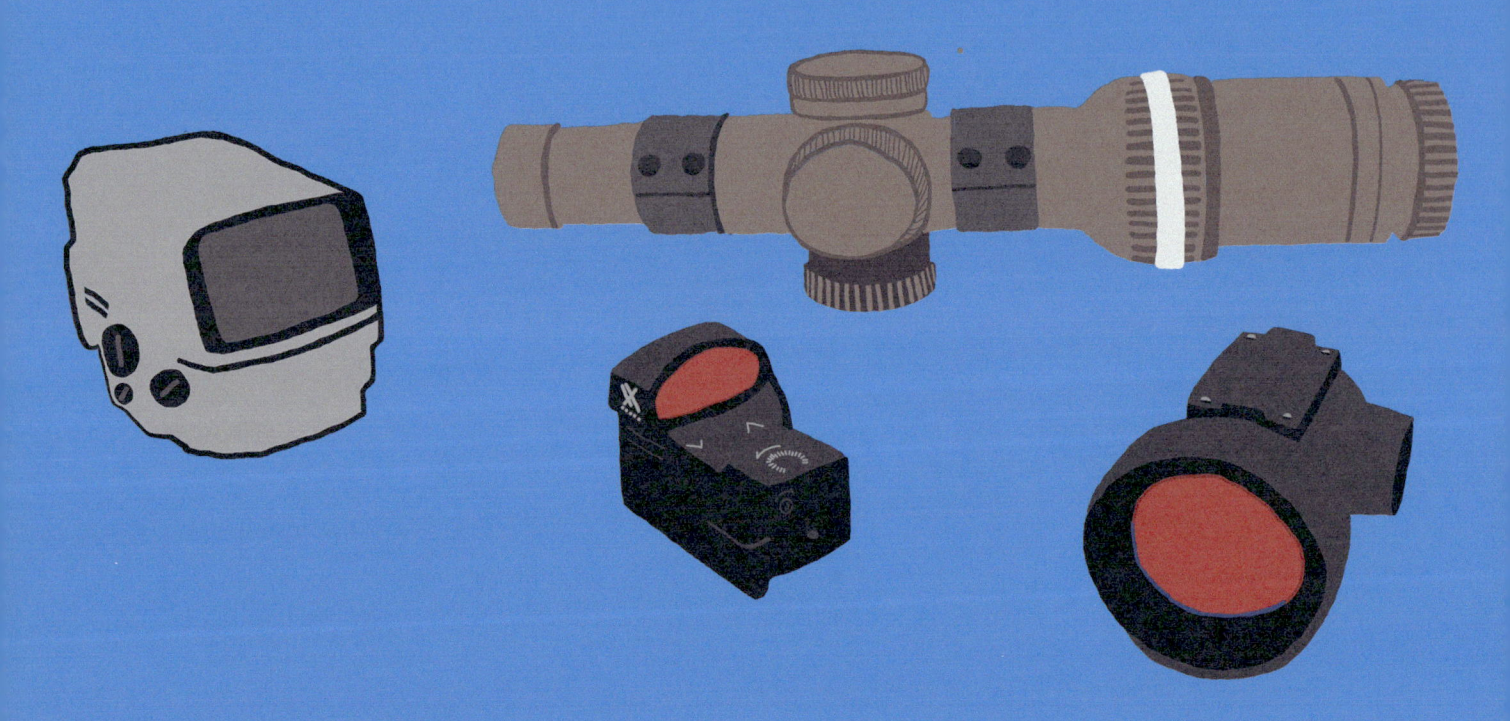

Pp
primers

Qq
qualify

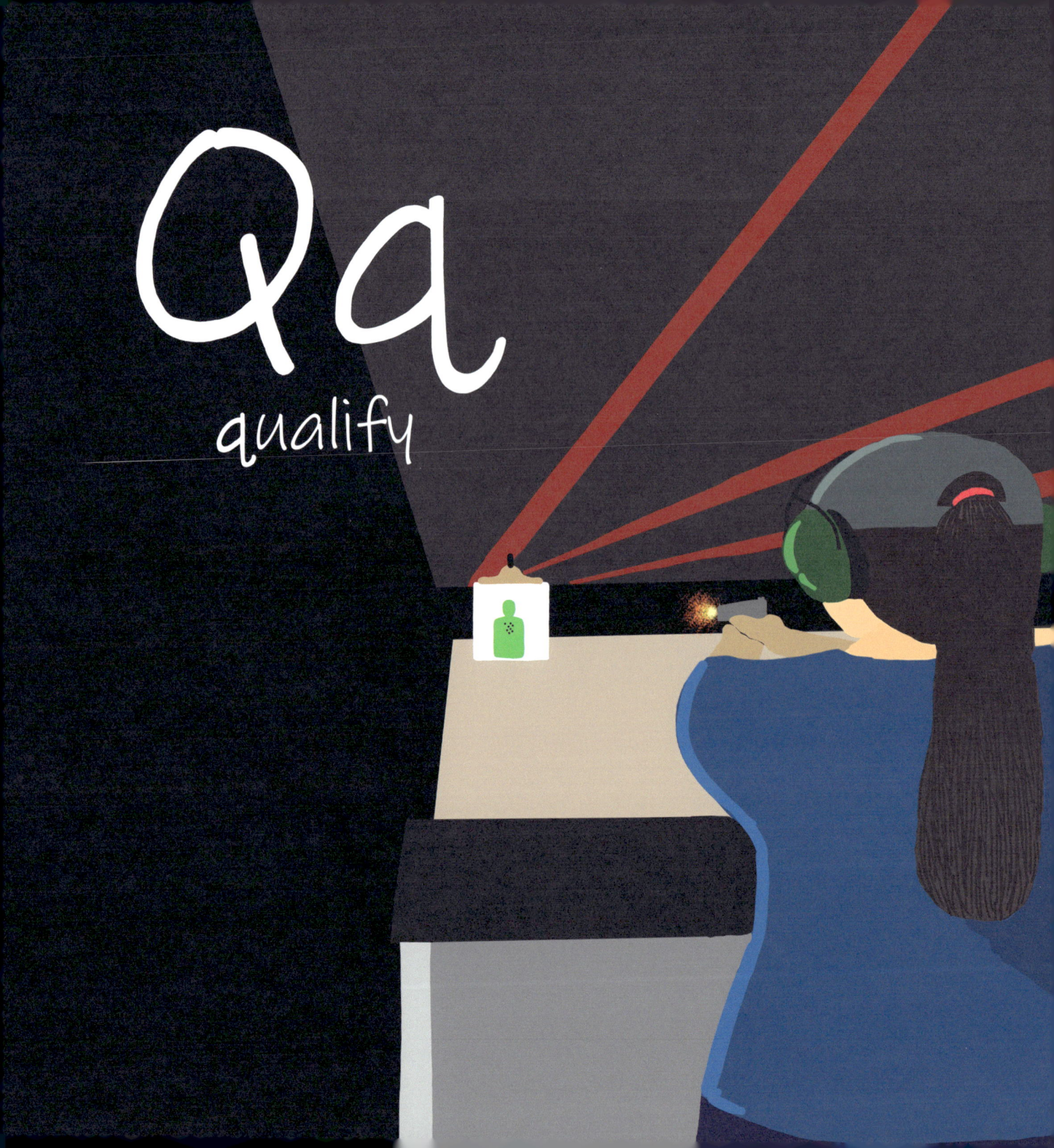

Rr
revolver

Ss sight, safety

finger off the trigger Tt

Uu
under supervision

Vv
venison

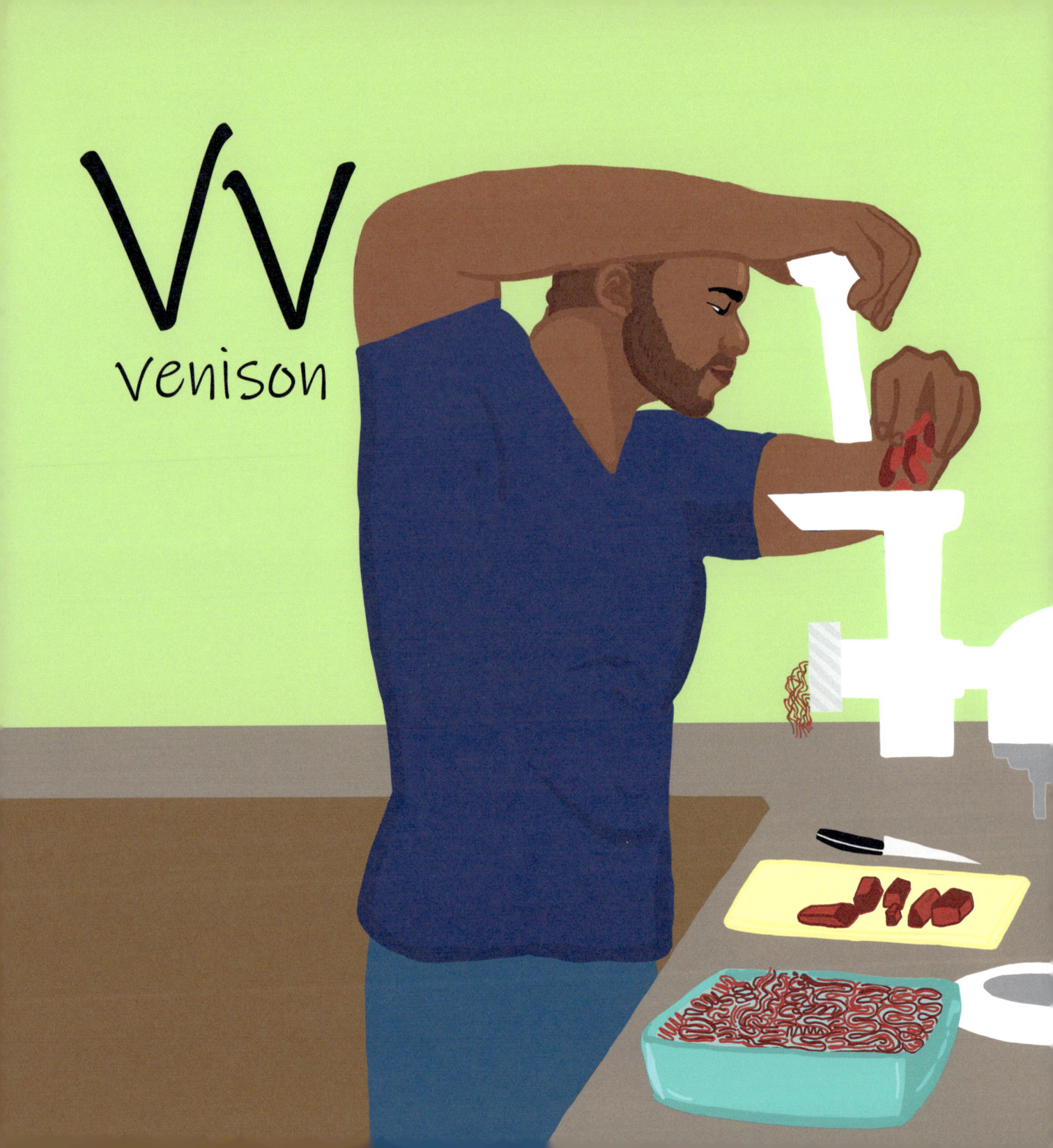

Ww
war is fought by real people

XX
x-ring

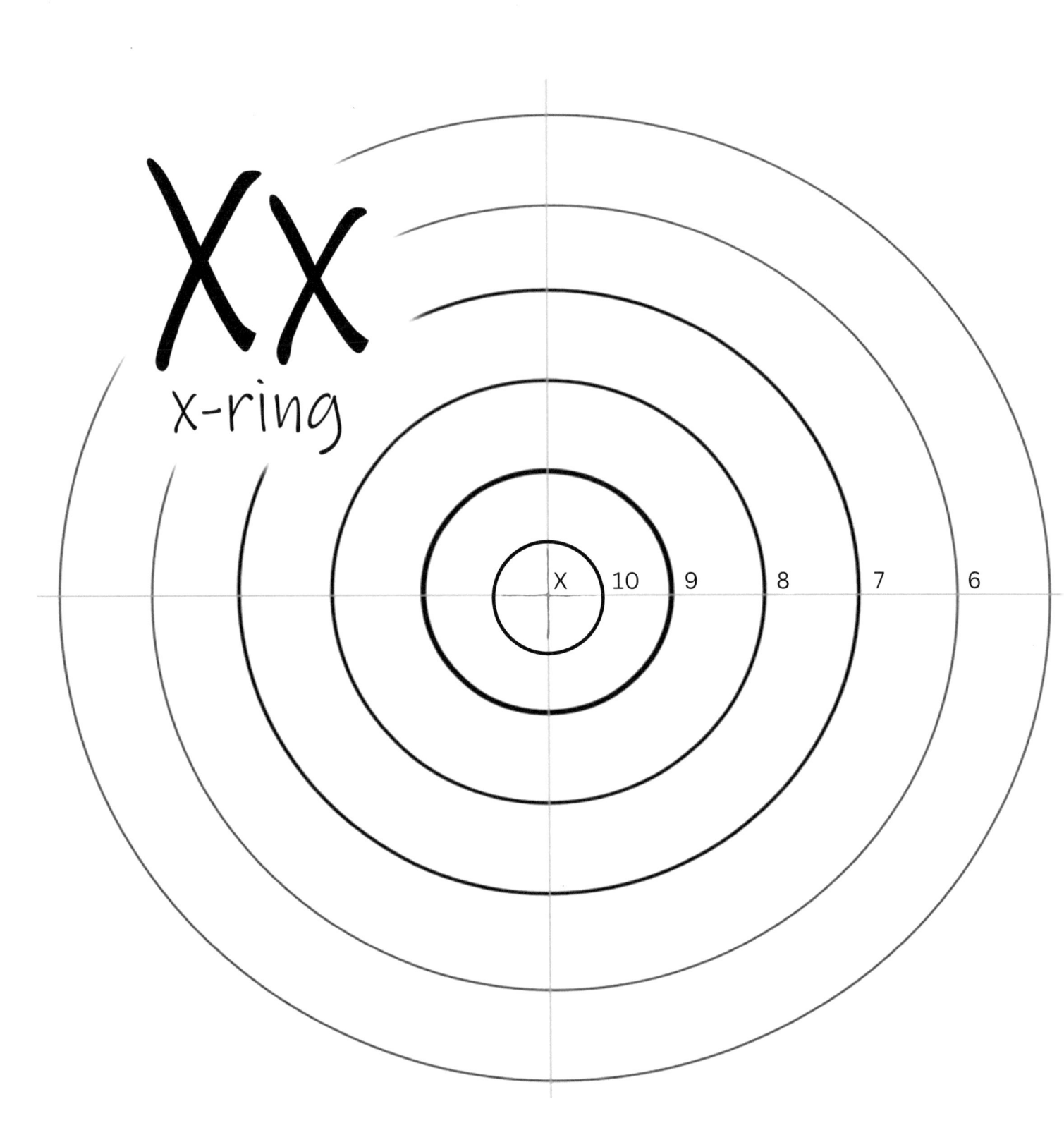

X 10 9 8 7 6

Yy youth sport shooting

Zzzzz

Sleep safely at night,
you won't be harmed.
Freedoms give might!
Your family is armed.

Expanding on the basics in Freedom Baby ABC, this activity book has pages that:

- Honor our six military branches
- Explain the Second Amendment principles our founding fathers valued
- What to bring to the range
- Firing positions for competitions
- Emphasize knowing what is beyond your target, and more

While it has coloring sheets and activities like crosswords and mazes, it also teaches the actual anatomy of a "pew," how primers work, the parts of a handgun, the similarities between different kinds of rifles, and much more! It's the perfect quiet activity for kids in deer blinds or for screen-free time on road trips. Parents will be glad to give the Gun Safety Activity Book for Kids to their older children because it builds on the six safety principles from Freedom Baby ABC.

PEEK inside!

scan this

Atrocious Idea!
Reviewed in the United State on July 17, 2021
I find this book **appalling.** To try and instill "gun culture" in a child is child **abuse**. It is basically brainwashing disguised as a children's book. Do not buy this book!

Sometimes, a one-star review from someone you disagree with is the same as an *endorsement!*

Go to Amazon and take a look at my 1-star reviews, left by people who hate liberty, just to lower the book's rating. Amazon Ads tags this safety book as "dangerous for children," making it difficult to advertise. If you enjoyed <u>Freedom Baby ABC</u>, please tell your friends about it. Post about it in on your social media and buy copies as gifts. And, please leave your own review. Ask a locally owned gun store if they would like to sell copies of either book- email me at greatbooks@janesharpe.com for wholesale purchases.

other books by Jane Sharpe include

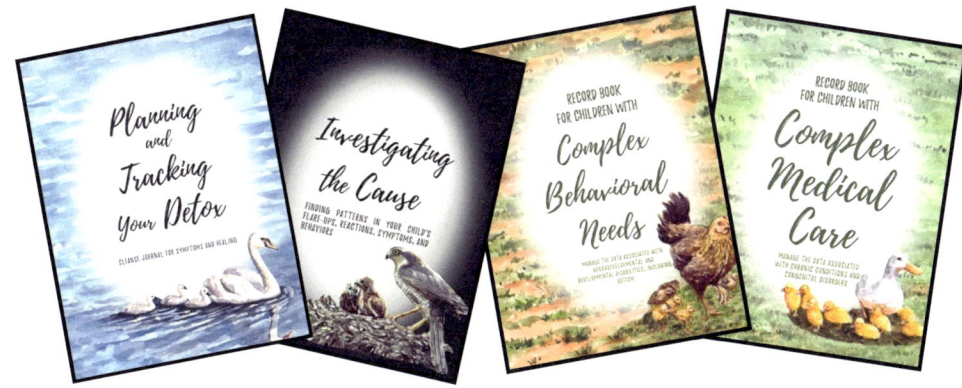

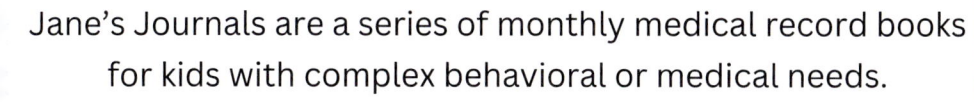

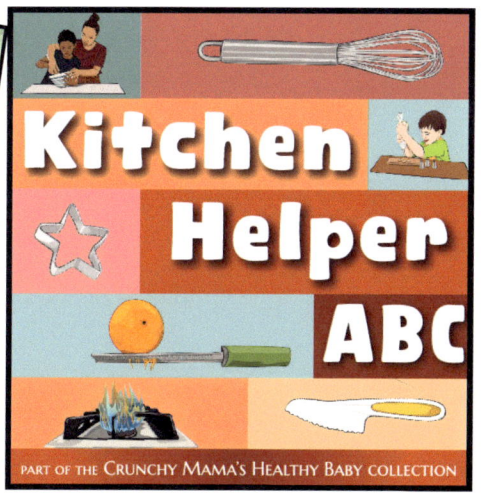

Jane's Journals are a series of monthly medical record books for kids with complex behavioral or medical needs.

Keep an eye out for *Winston, the Cat in a Mech Suit*

A sleepy kitty.

A house full of chores.

With a family's frustrating feline getting in the way, how will tasks get done?

The family can't bear to wake Winston the ginger cat, even when he's in the way! It looks like nothing will get accomplished… until he steps into his mech suit. Follow Winston in his sci-fi suit as he does all the chores that he blocked when he was napping!

Scan this QR code or go to www.JaneSharpe.com so you can keep up-to-date with all the upcoming books!

Made in the USA
Columbia, SC
19 March 2025